Network Marketing Success

27 Things You Should Know About Network Marketing and What It Really Takes to Become Set for Life.

T.J. Rohleder

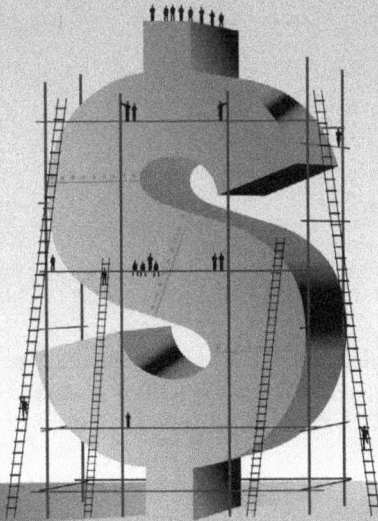

VOL.
#2

Disclaimer: This book is for information only. No specific results are implied or guaranteed. No ethical and honest person can promise or guarantee that you'll make any sum of money in network marketing or any business model. It's up to you to decide how you choose to act on this information. The bonus section of this book tells you about a unique network marketing opportunity. If interested, you'll be invited to call a recorded hotline and request a Special Report with the details.

Terence Storm Publishing
P.O. Box 198
Goessel, Kansas 67053

ISBN 1-933356-59-6

Introduction

Susan Sly was diagnosed with a terrible autoimmune disease in 2000. At her lowest point, she was scraping by as a single mother while sleeping on her brother-in-law's sofa. Scratching and clawing for every dollar, she barely made ends meet during those lean times. At her lowest, she had to tell her son he couldn't go to a friend's birthday party because she could not afford to buy him a small gift. She was not just broke. She was suicidal, and she was desperate.

Through a persistent friend, she got her start in the industry you'll read about in this short book. In her first year, she brought in $50,000. Her income climbed to $180,000 in her second year... $450,000 in year 3... $680,000 by her 4th year. In her best year so far, she brought in more than $2 million dollars.

"Formal education will make you a living;
self-education will make you a fortune."
— *Jim Rohn*

Would you like to make up to $500 a day... every day? Or more than that? How about $1,000 a day? Or as much as $1,000,000 a year?

Does that sound like pie in the sky?

Too good to be true?

A fantasy you can only dream about?

It is for most people. But not the people who are using the secrets in this book. People who are now making up to $500 a day and much, much more. Some who are making as much as $50,000 to $100,000 a month and even more.

Too good to be true? No, this is the truth!

Imagine that. These people started with very little money and are now making up to $500 to $1,000 a day... and even more.

But that's not all. It gets even better! In this little book, you will discover the proven, simple, and powerful ways to make the most money and achieve more of the success you always wanted.

"The two most important requirements for major success are: first, being in the right place at the right time, and second, doing something about it"
— *Ray Kroc*

Not only have average people discovered how to make up to $500 a day or even more, but...

- They're doing it their way.

- They choose who they're going to work with, and who they will for.

- They call their own shots.

- They have the freedom to do whatever they want, and they are making all the money they want and need.

- They have learned the secrets that produce big financial success.

These people are living the ultimate dream come true! This dream is their reality. **Their secret:** these people have discovered how to make money in the network marketing business.

This is one of the most proven ways to become financially set for life.

The network marketing industry is over 70 years old. We have been researching and investigating various network marketing opportunities for decades. We have seen them all. We've examined every inch of it from the top down. And we've seen a large and growing number of average people make up to $500 to $1,000 a day and even more. There's no better way for the average person to make money. **Here's why...**

- You choose your own hours.

- You can make money while having plenty of time to spend with your friends and family.

- You can do it all online and/or offline.

- You will be in business for yourself, but never by yourself.

"The future of network marketing is unlimited. There's no end in sight. It will continue to grow, because better people are getting into it. They are raising the entire standard of MLM to the point where soon, it will be one of the most respected business methods in the world."
— *Brian Tracy*

You can become financially set for life, if you're willing to do the things we'll tell you about in this book.

This book may have been given to you as a gift. If so, it could be the greatest gift you've received in your entire life! **That may sound a bit over the top, but what we are about to share with you is a proven way to make as much as $5,000 to $50,000 a month or more in your own home-based business.** We'll teach you the right way to make money in network marketing.

I started this Introduction with the story of Susan Sly. But there are many other amazing network marketing success stories. Here are a few of my favorite:

>> **Denice and Tom Chenault** make over $1 million a year with no employees, no big office, no infrastructure, and no warehouse full of inventory. They report that other people in their company are earning over a million a year, too.

>> **Gloria Mayfield Banks** will tell you why she left her $65,000 a year job at IBM to go into the network marketing business, and how she's generated over $10,000,000 in this business.

>> **Brian Carruthers** is one of the least assuming people you'll meet. You'd never pick him out of a lineup of millionaires. And yet, Brian has made over $15,000,000 in the network marketing business.

>> **Brandon and Lynette Cunningham** share their deeply personal story on this video. Toward the end, you'll hear how they're able to take several months off and their $80,000 a month in passive

income keeps coming to them.

>> **Frank Marone and Joe Occhiogrosso** made good money in the insurance business before the financial market crashed in 2008. They had 15 employees and monthly expenses of $40,000 to $50,000. Pressures mounted to keep their insurance business afloat. Then they discovered network marketing. Now, they make millions of dollars a year, without the employees, without offices, without the headaches and hassles of a typical business.

>> **Jeff Roberti** has earned over $80 million dollars in network marketing. The most amazing thing is how humble he is. Do a search for him and the other network marketing superstars I have just mentioned.

These stories [and many more online] are meant to inspire you and show you what's possible in this industry. These are top earners in the industry and their results are certainly atypical. They are not meant to indicate that you will earn anywhere near these amounts of money. And they definitely prove that anyone has the potential to become financially set for life in this industry. I do hope you'll take the time to study this small book and go online and find more of these amazing success stories to inspire you. *And with all that said, let's begin...*

27 Things You Should Know About Network Marketing and What It <u>Really</u> Takes to Become Set for Life.

#1. Network marketing is a personal sales and distribution business (or channel).

Network marketing is a distribution model for companies who have products they want to sell and don't want to go through traditional distribution channels. They set up a network of independent distributors (average people – not executive middlemen) who help them promote their products to the marketplace, primarily using word of mouth advertising.

#2. This industry is huge!

The network marketing industry produces almost 200 billion a year in worldwide revenue. This is a booming industry that's growing by leaps and bounds! The commissions paid out to the sales reps and the distributors who are helping those companies distribute their products is about $200 million every day.

#3. This is <u>not</u> a pyramid scheme.

This industry gets a bad name because of a few bad people. Like all industries, a few bad apples spoil the bunch. But most of its terrible reputation doesn't come from this small group; it comes from the larger group of good and well-meaning

<u>people</u> <u>who</u> <u>don't</u> <u>really</u> <u>understand</u> <u>the</u> <u>business</u> <u>they're</u> <u>in</u>.

The average newcomer to this business gets started after they attend an "opportunity meeting" or watch a series of online presentations. Many of them are so thrilled about the money-making potential of this business model, they believe they will **make a fortune overnight!**

New distributors get very excited about this amazing business, and some of them tend to exaggerate. They are so passionate! They get excited about the huge amounts of money that others have already made and are earning each month, and it drives them wild with excitement!

"The successful networkers I know, the ones receiving tons of referrals and feeling truly happy about themselves, continually put the other person's needs ahead of their own."
— *Bob Burg*

This leads some of these well-intentioned people to say things they shouldn't say...

- They tell people it's simple and easy to make a fortune, when it's not. This is an entrepreneurial venture, not a get-rich scheme. Entrepreneurship isn't always easy, and it requires a new set of skills to master it.

- They say the money will come pouring in super fast. It often takes time to grow your new business.

- They say the products sell themselves. They

don't. If that were true, the companies wouldn't need you and other distributors.

- They tell prospects that their products can cure things they can't. They try to convince others that their products are magical.

Most of these claims are pure exaggeration.

<u>Unfortunately, many newcomers believe these things</u>. They get involved in this business, believing all of these exaggerated claims. **Then, when they don't get the instant results they've been led to believe they should get, they give up.** Many of the people who quit blame their lack of success on the false belief that the network marketing business they were involved with was some kind of illegal 'pyramid scheme' or something like that, instead of the real reasons, which is the fact that they were never given a true understanding of this business model to begin with.

"We're in the midst of a boom in home-based businesses, and it shows no sign of slowing."
— *Paul Zane Pilzer*

#4. The big money is made by building your own sales and distribution team.

Everyone in this business gets paid on the sale of products and services. There is no other way.

You must move the products and services your company

provides through your own distribution system. **The large sums of money are made by building a network of other people who are doing the same thing.** You can sell the products at retail and make a high commission. Or you can build a team of others who sell the products and you earn a smaller commission, but through a larger network of people.

It's the combined sales through the larger group of people that gives you the leverage that others have used to make as much as $30,000 to $50,000 and even $100,000 a month or more. However, the thing to realize is that nobody makes any money <u>until</u> <u>and</u> <u>unless</u> the products are sold.

#5. This is a business where a lot of people each do a little.

You are paid a commission on the sale of products and services that are made throughout your sales organization. It's a lot of people, each doing a small amount of retailing the products and recruiting others. One of the richest people in the world once said: *"I'd rather have 1% of 100 people's efforts than 100% of my own efforts."* That's the right way to think about network marketing. It's the secret to making a fortune!

#6. Why the companies are happy to share their profits with a big network of distributors.

Network marketing is word of mouth marketing on fire! Companies choose this method of distribution because it's so efficient, compared with traditional distribution channels. Think about the high costs and frustrations with traditional marketing and distribution channels today. The different voices. People who are pounding on you from every direction to try to get your attention; to get you to look at their ads and sales messages; to lure you into watching their videos or listening to whatever it is they want to say.

We have become really good at tuning out the endless assault of marketing messages that bombard us everyday. And these same problems exist within all levels of the supply chain.

Todays marketplace is so fragmented. Nobody's listening. Everyone is blocking out all of the advertising and marketing messages. **But all of this is causing word of mouth advertising to be more effective than ever.** One person who says, *"Hey, there's something I tried and it's really working for me,"* is going to sell somebody much more effectively than one hundred paid advertisements and all the ads on the internet.

#7. The more you learn, the more you can earn.

The most important thing to learn in this business is how to build and maintain relationships. The professionals in the network marketing business strive to educate people to the point that they understand what they have. And in order to educate them, you must communicate with them.

The skills that are required are very simple. First, you must connect with a person. You have to build rapport, build a little bit of trust, and through that process, you now have an entry point to educate them. **It's all very low key:** *"Here's my product, here's how it could help you, please check it out and let's see if this is right for you."* We determine if there's a need. If there is, great! We get them signed up as distributors in the business, or as retail customers for our products.

#8. Millions of new people are joining this industry every year.

The network marketing industry is exploding! More people want to be their own boss than at any other time in history. Downsizing has forced people into self-employment. Technology is wiping out jobs. It's wiping out entire industries. Human labor value is going down as technology goes up, and people are saying, *"I don't want to be a cog in some other system anymore. I want to be my own boss!"*

But there's one major problem: They don't know the best way to do it.

Here are a few of the problems you'll face when you try to start your own business:

- Where do I find a really great product?

- Do I have enough money to get started?

- **Who will help me succeed?**

- Who do I turn to if I get in over my head?

- **Who will be there to guide me through the**

rough times?

- Do I have the expertise to run my own successful business? What if I don't? Who do I turn to for help?

- **How will I stay competitive?**

- And many more concerns...

A good network marketing company has the answer to these questions.

"If I had to do it all over again, rather than build an old style type of business, I would have started building a network marketing business."
— *Robert T. Kiyosaki*

Network marketing is one of the only ways the average person can start their own business without a lot of risk. Today, there are over 100 million network marketing distributors worldwide. **This business is quickly losing the stigma that was attached to it in the past.** Those of us who are in this business love it because everything is put together for us. All we have to do is promote the products and services and build our sales organization. This makes it simple and virtually risk-free.

#9. How the network marketing industry competes with Amazon.com and other large retailers.

Amazon.com and the other huge retailers seem to be taking

over the world. This small group of giant companies are changing the way many people buy all kinds of products and services.

But what they don't have is true word of mouth advertising.

They may have a 'rating' system where people can leave their reviews and comments. **But they don't have a network of passionate people who believe in the product enough to share it with others.** Network marketing provides an important educational need in the marketplace. We educate people on products that will be valuable to them. We don't really deal with commodities as much. We just deal with exciting products that are valuable and we can help to inform others about.

"No matter what your product is, you are ultimately in the education business. Your customers need to be constantly educated about the many advantages of doing business with you, trained to use your products more effectively, and taught how to make never-ending improvement in their lives."
— *Robert G. Allen*

#10. The best way to build this business.

I have mastered a very unique marketing method called 'direct response marketing.' This is a powerful method we use to pre-qualify prospective customers and distributors, before we even talk with them about the business.

This gives you 3 key advantages:

A.   It brings the highest quality people to you, already pre-sold and ready to go!

B. <u>It eliminates the need to bother people.</u>

C. The people who are most interested will see your information and contact you.

<u>With this marketing method, the very best prospects come to you, asking you for more information.</u> This is the best way to build this business because the only people that you and your team will be talking with are people who are already educated and eager to know more.

Another strong variation of this method is to hand out or mail a book like this one to a potential prospect. Get it into their hands. Then tell them you'll contact them in a few days to see if they want to know more. This is a simple and non-intrusive way to approach people. It's low-key and it really works!

People don't want to feel high-pressured. Most of the people you give or mail this book to will see it as a positive thing. Now they're ready and willing to hear more of what you have to offer them. This is the easy and best way to build your business. See the Bonus Section at the end of this book for more details.

"What you sow, you reap. It's a law of nature.
Network marketing is perfectly aligned with that.
You get truly, EXACTLY what you're worth!
No nepotism, no favoritism. That's rare today."
— *Bob Proctor*

#11. Strive to be a true professional.

Many newcomers to this business are searching for a way to make something from nothing. These people get in... cross their fingers... and hope for the best. **They treat this business as if it's a lottery scheme.** They almost always fail.

To succeed in the biggest way, you must strive to be a professional. Learn some skills, give it some time. Your effort will be rewarded. It takes some time and some effort to achieve success, but it will be worth it. Set proper expectations and go out there and show the world that network marketing isn't perfect, but if you have an entrepreneurial bone in your body, it may be the ultimate way to make money! This beats every other entrepreneurial venture for the average person, bar none, but you must strive to be a professional and treat it as a real business.

#12. The world's greatest way to make full time money with a part-time business.

Having your own business is the American dream. But this dream becomes a nightmare for many who do it. They suffer from endlessly long hours, high stress, and low returns. **The failure rate of a small business is very high. The pay can be embarrassingly low.** Many small business owners continue to struggle to make a profit after deducting all of their costs for leasing, inventory, staff, and operations. The answer is network marketing: An opportunity to own your own business without the burden of doing everything yourself.

An entrepreneur's dream come true!

As an independent representative (also known as a distributor, affiliate, associate, consultant, member, or business owner) you form a partnership with a corporation who provides a product or service, along with administrative and marketing support.

- The corporation takes care of the back end of the business for you.

- **This frees you up to focus on the part of the business that can produce instant income.**

- Your income comes from selling products or services, and from recruiting others to help promote the products or services.

- **The higher your total team sales, the higher your income.**

This is an amazing part-time business because it costs almost nothing to start and very little to run. You're in business for yourself, but never by yourself. You can choose your own hours, make lots of money, and have plenty of time to do the things in life that are most important to you.

#13. You can make money right away.

Network marketing is one of the few businesses where you can earn as you learn. Some people make huge sums of money right out of the gate. If you find yourself faltering, do this:

- Think of the millions of people who labor through years of university or college for a chance to join the ranks of the higher-income earners. Some

17

achieve financial independence, but many never do.

- Visualize the millions who invest their own money in a business, only to end up working 14 to 18 hours a day, trying to make it pay against all odds.

- Think about all of the people who waste their precious lives stuck in traffic, as they commute to the office and back.

- Become aware of all of the people who miss the important events in their life, and the people they love, due to work commitments.

- Consider all the people who hate their boring, repetitive, soul-sucking jobs. Polls indicate over 85% of workers are unhappy with their jobs.

Focus on these things. Then think of how lucky you will be when you're at the helm of your own low-risk, high-reward business. A business where you have the freedom to decide how your time will be spent and the people you will spend it with.

With all that in mind, consider this...

For well under $1,000, you can start a business that's making many people a small fortune.

If you are prepared to move out of your comfort zone and commit to making it work, whatever your current situation, you can join the hundreds of thousands of people who are making money and living a dream lifestyle from their network marketing business. This is wealth in the true spirit of the word.

"When I read in Fortune magazine that Warren Buffet, the billionaire investor and one of the world's richest men, was investing in a direct sales (network marketing) company, I decided I was missing something."
— *David Bach*

#14. It takes discipline and focus to succeed.

The amount of money you make in this business depends on you and what you do. Not everyone succeeds in this business, but that's true of all things.

Many people get involved in all types of enterprises and don't do anything. This includes the fact that many people go to college for 4 to 6 years or more and never do anything with their college degree. Plus, we discovered that a full 90% of new licensed real estate agents never sell a single home. When we learned that, we were shocked!

Unfortunately, an alarming number of people simply **lack the discipline to finish whatever they start.** Think about it; most people who buy a book don't read it from cover-to-cover. The book is sitting on their shelf, but they haven't read the whole thing. The same thing's true in this industry. There are people who get involved in network marketing and never take the next step. Because the price of entry is so low, it makes it easy to quit. You don't want to be that person, and now you don't have to be.

#15. How to approach friends and family.

Most people start with their family and friends because these are the people who know and trust you. We recommend a very specific approach that will show them the respect they deserve. Here's how it works: you simply give them a book like the one you're reading, and then tell them you'll follow up with them in a few days. This will open their mind about the network marketing business, and help them understand what they don't know. Then all you have to do is follow up with them and see if they liked what they read. It's simple. It's easy. And best of all, it's a low pressure approach that gets proven results!

This same book can also be given to people you meet. Just purchase a few copies of this book. Then give it away to people you think may be interested, then collect their contact information and call them in a few days. When you call them, simply ask what they liked about the book and answer any questions they have. In some cases, you won't have to call them, because they'll reach out to you first!

Once you have the conversation started, everything gets so much easier.

✔ From that point forward, you'll know if they're open and receptive and want to know more.

✔ If so, you can help them try your products or enroll on your team, and then teach them how to do what you're doing.

✔ This book is a great ice-breaker! It may be the ultimate non-intrusive way to recruit new distributors into your team.

✔   Plus, those who do not become distributors can become retail customers for your products.

With this approach, you'll never high-pressure anyone. Just hand or mail them this great little book and let it open their minds to this amazing industry. Then, follow up with them and see if there's any interest. If so, great! You just introduced them into your products and the unique network marketing opportunity, and you did it in a way that didn't offend anyone. If not, you will both be happy about the fact that you took this low-key approach, because you gave them an easy way to tell you they are not interested.

"Network marketing is based purely on relationship selling, which is the state of the art in selling today. Small and large companies throughout the country and the world are realizing that individuals selling to their friends and associates is the future of sales, because the critical element in buying is trust."
— *Brian Tracy*

#16. Find a company with a line of products that excites you!

The people who make the most money in this business (and we want that list to include you) have found companies and products they're passionate about. They have <u>enthusiasm</u> for the products and the distribution model; that is, network marketing itself. Remember this: the last four letters in the word "enthusiasm" – IASM – are an acronym for "<u>I am sold myself!</u>"

You must genuinely be sold on the fact that your products, the company behind them, and their network marketing opportunity are the very best, or you will never succeed at the highest level.

The good news is the fact that **your beliefs can be built and strengthened.** In other words, it's your job to discover all the ways your products can help people, plus all the money they can potentially earn by offering these products or services to other people. Do this well, and your belief and passion will convince others they can share in the benefits and great financial opportunity.

#17. What to do when someone says no.

Oftentimes, people say "no" because the approach was wrong or the timing wasn't right. A few weeks or months from now, if you find creative ways to stay in touch, they could suddenly be ready to get more information and maybe get started. We've seen it hundreds of times. The secret is to use low pressure methods of staying in touch with people and continuing to let them know that you are here if and when they're ready to take the next step.

#18. Network marketing is built on long-term relationships.

This is a whole different approach to sales and marketing. For example, if you sell somebody a used car, the relationship is generally over when the customer drives off the car lot. **Not so in network marketing. We intentionally stay connected.** We stay in contact. We keep the conversation going. If more sales people did that with their customers and clients, they'd experience far greater success. Most salespeople only call their prospects and customers when they need the business. Long term relationship building, the growing of a network of people who know you, like you, and trust you, is one of the most valuable things you can do. This business model gives you the ultimate way to make money with this important marketing principle.

#19. How to profit from social media.

Many network marketers have cracked the code of how to recruit through social media. They taught themselves how to use the social media platforms in a way that doesn't offend others. It's been a revolution because...

- **You can reach your best prospects with a click of a button.**

- You can find these people anywhere in the world. For example, if you're interested in fitness, you can find every fitness group in the world and begin to have a conversation with those people.

- This makes it simple and easy to communicate to the right people and see if your product or opportunity might be a solution for them.

If you like social media, this can be the best way to find your perfect audience. Even if you're living in a tiny little town where you don't know anybody and many of your friends and family have already said *"I'm not interested,"* you have the entire world at your fingertips.

"The fastest way to get rich in life is
to solve other people's problems."
— *Mike Dillard*

#20. How the network marketing company helps you make the maximum sum of money.

The network marketing company you choose will do many things to help ensure that you have the best opportunity to get paid the largest sum of money.

- They take care of the research, development, and packaging of the products.

- They make sure that you and everyone on your team gets paid on time, every time.

- They make the products and the opportunity available around the world. This lets you do business in many different countries if you choose to.

- They have legal teams who deal with red tape, bureaucracy, and compliance issues.

- They are responsible for the majority of the customer service work.

- They give you the framework to operate your business from anywhere in the world, and have customers from anywhere in the world.

"Somebody, somewhere is looking for your opportunity, and you're afraid to tell them. Your fear is robbing them of a blessing."
— *Darryl Van Kirk*

In short, **the company takes care of all of the headaches and hassles that you would normally be forced to do in your own business.** Plus, they host events, provide tools and training, and many other important things that are designed to help you experience the highest levels of success.

All you do is promote the products and build a team of others who do the same. You're paid on the productivity of your entire team. If you're a decent leader and you can get your team to be more productive, you can earn unlimited money. How much money could you make? Read on! The answer will surprise you, to put it mildly.

#21. You must think like an entrepreneur.

Most people have always been paid by the hour. This causes them to think like an employee. But entrepreneurs think differently. **Our financial success comes from building a group of customers or joint-venture business partners who continue to do business with us.** For example, a successful restaurant may have hundreds of customers who keep coming back, year after year, and ultimately introduce the restaurant to their friends and family (who do the same). This large group of repeat customers ends up making successful owners tremendous sums of additional money.

A successful business will take some time to build. Once you build it, you have the power to become financially set for life. But to think like an entrepreneur means you must accept the fact that a successful business takes some time and effort to grow, before the riches can come to you. The same is true of network marketing. If you put in the time and some effort, you can be greatly rewarded.

#22. Many people expect something for nothing.

Many newcomers to this business industry love the idea of having other people who make money for them. But what they're really searching for is someone to do everything for them. There's a difference. <u>Don't</u> <u>make</u> <u>this</u> <u>mistake</u>. Network marketing can pay you massive sums of money through the efforts of other people, but the amount you make will always depend on you and what you do to build your team. Your team can make you financially free, but first you must build your team and customer base.

Understand this: Many people (who are no different than you) are getting paid up to $50,000 to $100,000 a month and even more in this industry. You have the power to do it, too! But you must expect to put in some time and effort to build your sales organization, before you reap this huge cash windfall. That may sound like common sense, and yet many people have unrealistic expectations and give up before they can build a solid team and make all the money that would and could be theirs. Make up your mind before you get started, that you will stay the course and work hard to achieve your financial goals.

"Network marketing is really the greatest source of grass-roots capitalism, because it teaches people how to take a small bit of capital, that is your time, and build the American dream."
— *Jim Rohn*

#23. The magic power of residual income.

Imagine how your life would be if you could take off for a month or two and keep getting huge sums of money. Think about how things could be if you could make money while shopping, sleeping, or spending quality time with family and friends. **How would your life change if the money you made had absolutely nothing to do with the number of hours you put in?** Well, that's what a steady and growing stream of residual income can do for you. Many of the richest people in the world use the wealth-building miracle of residual income, and so can you.

- With this type of income, the amount of money you make has little or even nothing to do with the amount of time and work you do.

- For the first time in your life you can be free to live the life you always wanted for yourself.

- You can shop, sleep, or vacation, and still get paid. You can enjoy your life while relaxing, and the money will keep flowing in.

This may sound like a dream, but it's not. It can be your reality. Millions of people all over the world have discovered how to tap into the power of residual income. **These people never have to worry about where their next dollar will come from – instead, they can relax and enjoy life, knowing that they are financially secure, no matter what.** And, here's the kicker: Many of these lucky people are network marketing distributors.

#24. You will cash-in from the power of "leveraged income".

There are 3 basic ways to make money:

1.   LINEAR INCOME: Sell your time for money.

This is the way 99% of the people make money. Everyone from day laborers who slave under the hot sun for minimum wage ... to brain surgeons who are paid thousands of dollars an hour. These people sell each hour of their time for a certain amount of money (a wage).

2.   DIRECT SALES INCOME: Sell a product or service.

With this second method, your money comes from sales of a product or service, not the amount of time you work. **This is a smarter way to make money.** In fact, the world is filled with millionaires who make their money with this second method.

But the real secret to getting rich is to use the final method...

3.   LEVERAGED INCOME: Let other people make you massive profits!

Selling products and services directly (the 2nd method) is quite capable of making you very rich. **But this third way to make money has made more people wealthy than the other two ways combined!** With this final method, you use the power of "leverage" to let other people make money for you... Once you set up the leveraged income system, all you do is sit back and cash the checks you receive.

Now for the best part: Network marketing lets you cash in with both the second and third ways to make money. You no longer need to get paid by the hour. This gives you the same type of power as the world's richest people.

"Network Marketing isn't perfect. It's just better."
— Eric Worre

#25. How to get started and succeed.

Other than getting back with the person who gave you this book, you must strive to understand and appreciate the amazing value the network marketing company can give you. **That's one of the main reasons we wrote this book.** We wanted to help you understand that, although network marketing isn't perfect and has its challenges, it's still so much better than any other form of entrepreneurship, because of all of the help and training you can receive. Just add it up and see if you agree...

- Consider everything we have said and you'll see: no other form of entrepreneurship for the average person can beat this.

- You must realize the outstanding type of opportunity you are now being invited into.

- Think deeply about everything we have said and

you'll begin to realize just how powerful and timely this type of opportunity is.

- Think about how exciting it is to be an entrepreneur, and how profitable it really can be. You will be in business and making money for yourself, but not by yourself.

- Then get involved in this business, develop some skills, and don't give up. You're going to love the big results you can achieve.

"If you are a person with big dreams and would love to support others in achieving their big dreams, then the network marketing business is definitely a business for you. You can start your business part-time at first and then as your business grows, you can help other people start their part-time business. This is a value worth having – a business and people who help others make their dreams come true."
— *Robert T. Kiyosaki*

Don't just cross your fingers and hope for the best. Choose the right company and develop some new skills, because **new skills build confidence and that confidence will lead to more action and more action will give you the results you want.** It's as simple as that. Not easy, but very simple.

The main thing is this: don't be an amateur who crosses their fingers and treats network marketing like a glorified lottery ticket. Don't just talk to a few people and hope that those people will sign up and do everything for you. If you've read this book, you know that kind of thinking is a recipe for failure. You don't want to fail. You want to succeed! You want to make a lot of money and have plenty of time to enjoy spending it.

And speaking of making a lot of money, that's the best part, and we saved for last.

#26. This business could potentially make you up to $1,000,000 a year or more!

Although it sounds hard to believe, there are people who are making over one million dollars a year in this business. One of our mentors once said, "I've reviewed countless company pay plans, and none of them have a ceiling. If you want to earn $1 million a week, no one can stop you – except you." The man who said this (Mark Yarnell) started broke and earned over $25 million dollars in the network marketing industry. There are many more like him. These people started for less than $1,000 and have made their fortune. Now you know the best way to join them.

#27. What it <u>really</u> takes to become set for life.

I saved the best news for last! It's the fact that newer and better network marketing companies give you the chance to cash-in without the headaches and hassles that others are forced to go through.

Network marketing is evolving. It's getting better in large part because newer and more innovative companies are doing these five things better. *They...*

1.   Help you make the largest sum of money in the fastest time.

2.   Do everything within their power to help the <u>newcomer</u> succeed.

3.   Create proven marketing systems that are easy to understand and simple to use.

4.   Let you make money <u>without</u> bothering family and friends.

5.   Do not require you to be a salesperson, public speaker, or social butterfly.

Compared to the older, well-established huge network marketing corporations, the people behind these newer types of companies care more about the average person – not just the heavy-hitters that bring them thousands upon thousands of new customers. **These are the network marketing opportunities of the future.** And thank God for the people behind them. Almost all of the people at the top of these newer types of network marketing companies are ex-distributors, including me. And the reason is because we understand the best aspects of this industry. The things that make it great. However, we also understand some of the major problems that stop the average person from making a great deal of money. We are deeply committed to developing the ultimate opportunity to help our distributors make big money without the headaches and hassles that most network marketing distributors (especially those who are involved in traditional network marketing companies) are forced to go through.

I hope you enjoyed this book. Please keep it in a safe place. Refer back to it often. And think deeply about all 27 of these powerful ideas. Plus, if you like this final idea, read the special Bonus Section for some exciting news.

<u>Bonus Section</u>

My Ultimate Network Marketing Discovery That Can Make You Financially Set for Life, with <u>NO</u> Phone Calls, <u>NO</u> Zoom Meetings, <u>NO</u> Long Hours, <u>NO</u> Personal Selling, <u>NO</u> Bothering Your Friends and Family, and <u>NO</u> Headaches and Hassles.

Thank you for reading my book. I ended it by telling you about some of the main ways that network marketing is evolving.

The new companies behind this evolution are striving to...

1. **Help you make the largest sum of money in the fastest time.**

2. Do all they can to help the newcomer succeed.

3. Create proven marketing systems that are easy to understand and simple to use.

4. **Let you make money – without bothering your family and friends.**

5. Not require you be a salesperson, public speaker, or social butterfly.

6. Truly care about the average person – not just the

heavy-hitters.

Almost all of these newer types of network marketing companies are attempting to do some of these 6 things well. But there are still gaps in their systems and holes in their compensation plans. In other words, they're not doing all six. However, in this Bonus Section, I'll tell you a few of the ways my company was built to do <u>all 6</u> of these things ... and more!

The secret: Our company is focused on helping **the average person get paid the largest amount of money in the fastest time.** We do not "pay deep" like traditional network marketing companies (paying small commissions that are divided out over large numbers of distributors). We do the exact opposite: We pay the **biggest** commissions to the **fewest** number of distributors. This makes our plan even more exciting, because it puts bigger commissions into our distributor's wallets even faster! After all, <u>making money right away is a major confidence booster</u>!

This gives you the ultimate way to make money with the powerful Direct Response Marketing secrets that made us millionaires. This is the most powerful way to stay home... <u>do a simple activity that can take just minutes a day</u> (that helps us attract new members)... and potentially make huge sums of money.

- ✔ I **guarantee** that all the hard work will be done for you.

- ✔ I **guarantee** this can make you all the money you want.

- ✔ I **guarantee** that you can make money in total privacy.

- ✔ I **guarantee** that this is perfect in good times or bad.

✔ I **guarantee** that this lets you stay home and make money, <u>without</u> the headaches and hassles that most network marketing distributors are forced to go through.

You will cash in with my rare and unusual secret method that has already generated a fortune for me and many other average people.

✔ You'll never have to do this for more than a few minutes a day.

✔ You can make money and have plenty of time to spend with your family and friends.

✔ This is private. Nobody has to know what you're doing to make money.

✔ You'll never do any personal selling or talk to anyone.

This lets you stay home – **DO NO HARD WORK** - and potentially get paid up to hundreds or thousands of dollars a month. That may sound hard to believe. But it's true. And when you know the secrets, you will be shocked!

Average folks from all walks of life have used the secrets we built into our new 'ascension model' to make more money than many Doctors and Lawyers.

And now, I have written a detailed new report to share the secrets behind this new discovery with you. And because you are reading this book, I'll rush it to you free, with no cost or obligation. It's called:

"The Low Cost Way to $1,000 a Day!"

This report is complete in every way. I think you'll love it! Just follow the simple instructions at the end of this section, and I'll RUSH it to you absolutely free. As you'll see: I've discovered a unique type of network marketing model with virtually no overhead. This can pay you commissions of **$500** ... **$1,000** ... and even **$3,000** for each sale that's made for you. **And that's only the start!** There's more! This business model is not 'traditional' Network Marketing. However, you can get paid huge commissions on big-ticket sales that we will gladly make for you and for other people who are placed into your Affiliate team. And now, with your permission...

I Will *RUSH* the Secrets to You.

My free report will reveal everything. It's yours with no cost or obligation. I can't promise or guarantee that you will make $1,000 a day or any specific sum (in this or any business model). However, you will receive my complete business plan that's based on a little-known secret that has generated millions of dollars for me and other average people. However, even though I can't guarantee any specific results, I will promise to show you how this gives you the potential to...

Make up to $100,000 to $250,000 a year and only put in a few short minutes a day.

The above statement may sound hard to believe. But once you let me help you get set up, it's possible for three reasons: **_FIRST_**, you can make extreme profit margins on core membership packages that we sell for you. **_SECOND_**, those memberships pay commissions of as much as $3,000 per sale. Just a few of those sales every month could add up to substantial sums of money! **_THIRD_**, you can also get paid for the sales we make for other people who we place into your Affiliate team. And **_FOURTH_**, our powerful marketing system and in-house sales team do the hard work for you, so all you do is put in minutes a day following our simple (and easy-to-use) system to help us attract new members. That's amazing, but true!

Not to brag, but I've brought in more than $150 million dollars with the core secret that my amazing 'ascension model' was built on. My proven marketing system does the selling for you. You spend just a few minutes following our simple system to help us attract new members. We take it from there. We'll spend our money on the expensive and difficult follow up marketing to convert those new prospects into members. Then, based on your level of qualification, we will pay you a generous commission for the membership sales we make for you and the people we place into your team.

My powerful 5-Level Ascension Model is the most proven way I know to help you gain true financial freedom. I've made millions with these secrets, and now I'm willing to help you cash-in with them, too. As you'll see, this is designed to...

<u>Help you become</u>
<u>financially set for life</u>!

This is a legal, moral, and ethical way to generate the

money you want. **Let me prove this to you.** Follow the instructions I'll give you in a moment. You'll receive my '**Low Cost Way to $1,000 a Day Report**' for no cost and no obligation. As you'll see, my rare and unusual method incorporates the very best aspects of network marketing, while eliminating the worst aspects. This fills a major gap in a rare and unusual trillion-dollar marketplace. **Very few know about this.** But the few who do know about this secret marketplace are making huge sums of money. Some have made millions. I am one of them. Now my secret can be yours at no cost.

I'm looking for a small group of Joint Venture business partners to make money with me. When you join me, I'll give you my proven turn-key System that's based on all I've done to generate millions of dollars. As you'll see, this amazing secret can change your life.

Along with this book, I've sent a copy of my new Special Report: "The Low Cost Way to $1,000 a Day."

Now that you've finished this book, please take a few more minutes to read through my Special Report. If your copy is missing – or you purchased this book from Amazon and it was shipped without the Special Report, let us know and we'll be happy to send you a copy.

My Special Report will give you more information about an opportunity to let me help you cash-in with the secrets I've shared with you in this book, through a unique Membership and Affiliate model. I'm looking for joint venture partners. So if you like what you read in the Special Report, let's connect. **I'd love to talk to you about how we can work together to help you achieve the success you've been searching for.**